Let's COOK!

Italy

The Culture and Recipes of Italy

Tracey Kelly

PowerKiDS
press™

Published in 2017 by
The Rosen Publishing Group, Inc.
29 East 21st Street, New York, NY 10010

Cataloging-in-Publication Data
Names: Kelly, Tracey.
Title: Culture and recipes of Italy / Tracey Kelly.
Description: New York : PowerKids Press, 2017. | Series: Let's cook! | Includes index.
Identifiers: ISBN 9781499431810 (pbk.) | ISBN 9781499432619 (library bound) | ISBN 9781499431827 (6 pack)
Subjects: LCSH: Cooking, Italian--Juvenile literature. | Food habits--Italy--Juvenile literature.
Classification: LCC TX723.K455 2017 | DDC 641.5945--dc23

For Brown Bear Books Ltd:
Text and Editor: Tracey Kelly
Editorial Director: Lindsey Lowe
Children's Publisher: Anne O'Daly
Design Manager: Keith Davis
Designer: Melissa Roskell
Picture Manager: Sophie Mortimer

Picture Credits: t=top, c=center, b=bottom, l=left, r=right. Front Cover: Shutterstock: lakov Kalinin c, neftali r, Ina Ts r, Viacheslav Lopatin r, wsf-s l, pingebat l, Noppasin t, milezaway t. Inside: 123rf: 29; Dreamstime: 28-29t, 33b, 35b, Paul Brighton 31b, Yulia Grigoryeva 36-37t, Eric Limon 28r, Gail Mikhalishina 19, Nick Nicko 8-9b, Nemanja Tomic 43, Vanilla Echoes 15b, 16b; Getty Images: Steve Delauw 37b, Viviane Ponti 38-39t, Thomas Tolstrup 31t; istockphoto: 27b; Shutterstock: 1r, 4tl, 4bl, 5r, 6bl, 20-21t, 20-21b, Leonid Andronov 5bl, 36, Arts Illustrated Studios 7b, Paola Bona 23t, 23br, Andreas Costos 5t, Paul Cowan 25, Mike Dotta 39c, Olga Gavrilova 6-7t, Claude Huot 38-39b, Andrea Izzottie 11br, K. Kulikov 22br, Victor Marigo 10-11t, Robert Milek 45, Lefteris Papaulakis 1bl, PFM Photosotck 22t, Pavel Siamionau 1l, Underworld 10bl; Thinkstock: AMZ Photo/istock 9tl, Digital Vision 30, Lesya Dolyuk 41, istockphoto 8-9t, Inga Nielsen/istock 17b.

Special thanks to Klaus Arras for all other photography.

Manufactured in the United States of America
CPSIA Compliance Information: Batch #BW17PK: For Further Information contact Rosen Publishing, New York, New York at 1-800-237-9932.

Contents

Looking at Italy

Located in southern Europe, Italy is home to 61 million people. The country is celebrated for its natural beauty, history, and mouthwatering food!

EUROPE

Italy

AFRICA

Italy sticks out into the Mediterranean Sea. It is bordered by France, Austria, Slovenia, and Switzerland.

Penne

Fusilli

Rigatoni

Strozzapreti

Spaghetti

Viva l'Italia!

People from all over the world look to Italy's vibrant community for inspiration. As well as its delicious cuisine, the country is famous for art, fashion, opera, architecture, and sports. Tourists pour into the country to soak up its unique culture. In Rome alone, over 4 million people per year visit its ancient landmarks, including the Pantheon, the Colosseum, and the Roman Forum. Many people also visit the Vatican, the seat of the Roman Catholic Church. But it's not just the cities that attract visitors. Italy's landscape offers an awe-inspiring range of scenery. It features miles of Mediterranean beaches and picturesque ports, with stunning mountains, rolling hills, and vineyards inland. Viva l'Italia (Long Live Italy)!

Italian pasta comes in many shapes and sizes.

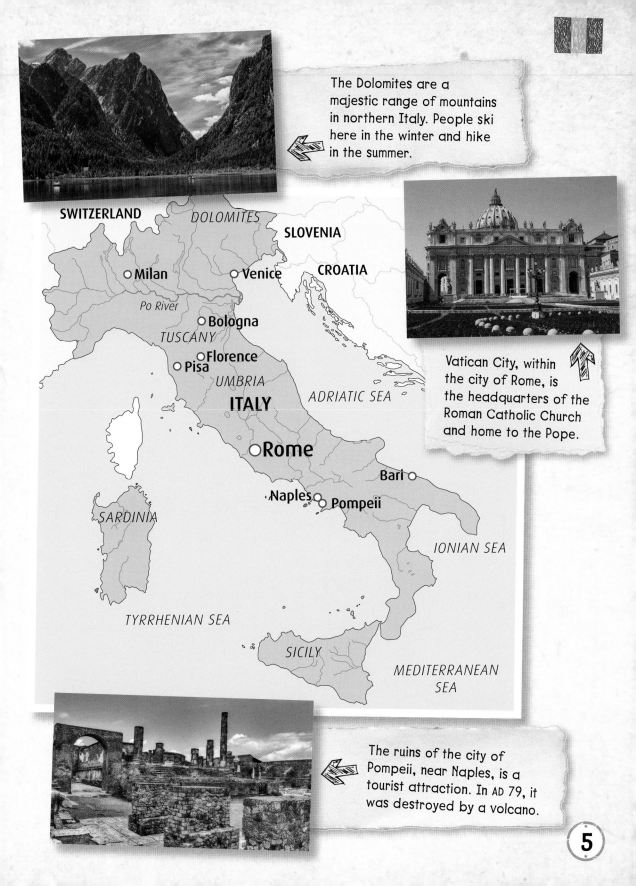

The Dolomites are a majestic range of mountains in northern Italy. People ski here in the winter and hike in the summer.

Vatican City, within the city of Rome, is the headquarters of the Roman Catholic Church and home to the Pope.

SWITZERLAND

DOLOMITES

SLOVENIA

CROATIA

Milan

Venice

Po River

Bologna

TUSCANY

Florence

Pisa

UMBRIA

ITALY

ADRIATIC SEA

Rome

Bari

Naples

Pompeii

SARDINIA

IONIAN SEA

TYRRHENIAN SEA

SICILY

MEDITERRANEAN SEA

The ruins of the city of Pompeii, near Naples, is a tourist attraction. In AD 79, it was destroyed by a volcano.

The North

The grand Dolomite Mountains lie in the northeast of Italy. Ski resorts, medieval castles, and picturesque towns nestle on its slopes. Venice is one of the most unusual cities in the world. Located in a lagoon in the Adriatic Sea, its "streets" are canals! In the northwest, the rocky Alps offer wild, untamed scenery. And on the coast near Genoa—where Christopher Columbus was born in 1451—is the Italian Riviera. People come here to sail, swim, and sunbathe on the beaches of the Mediterranean Sea.

 Portofino is a resort town on the beautiful Italian Riviera, in the north of Italy.

Medieval towns such as Abeto dot the hillsides in Umbria, in central Italy.

Central Italy

The heart of Italy features the regions of Tuscany and Umbria, which have beautiful, rolling hills and fertile valleys. Museums in Florence are packed with some of the most famous paintings in the world. The Uffizi Gallery holds Sandro Botticelli's masterpieces, *The Birth of Venus* and *Spring.* Nearby Pisa is home to the 12th-century Leaning Tower. But it is Italy's capital, Rome, that draws visitors in droves. Some of its buildings—such as the Colosseum—date back 2,000 years. Rome also has elegant parks, stunning churches—and some of the best cuisine in Italy!

Southern Italy

Magnificent mountains and scenic coastlines make up much of southern Italy. Calabria, the peninsula that forms the "toe" of Italy's bootlike shape in southwest Italy, is surrounded by crystal-clear blue seas. Vineyards and orchards lie on the lower slopes of its rugged mountains, with forests and rocky highlands above. Puglia, to the southeast, has vineyards, ancient farmland, and unique architecture, with *trulli*, cone-roofed houses.

The island of Sicily is home to Mt. Etna, Europe's tallest volcano at 10,922 feet (3,330 meters). Many ancient Greek ruins are dotted around Sicily. From 1880 to 1920, around 3 million people from southern Italy emigrated to the United States to seek a better life.

DID YOU KNOW?

Latin is the language that was spoken in ancient Rome. It was used for centuries by educated people. The Romance languages, such as French, Italian, Spanish, Portuguese, and Romanian, all grew out of Latin.

Mt. Etna, an active volcano, towers above Taormina, a town on the east coast of Sicily.

Food and Farming

With its rolling hills, wide plains, racing rivers, and sunny weather, Italy has the perfect conditions to grow nutritious food.

Healthy Diet

The Mediterranean diet is believed to be one of the healthiest in the world. People who eat fresh, colorful vegetables and fruit, garlic, olive oil, fish, and nuts are said to live longer and healthier lives than those who have meat-heavy diets. Farmers grow a variety of garlic, peppers, tomatoes, eggplants, zucchini, arugula, olives, and onions. Citrus fruits, such as oranges and lemons, are also grown in the south. Fresh produce is available at markets in most small villages and big cities alike.

The coastal waters surrounding Italy are teeming with fish and shellfish. Fishermen near Puglia catch octopus, shrimp, scallops, and oysters for fresh seafood dishes. Sicilians also enjoy swordfish, snapper, and cuttlefish.

An Italian market sells a huge selection of colorful, fresh vegetables and fruit.

A specially trained pig digs for prized truffles in a forest in northwestern Italy.

Meat and Mushrooms

Farmers raise cattle for beef, milk, and cheese in the Dolomite Mountains in the north. The high meadows are perfect grazing areas for the cows in summer. Crops are also grown, and hay is cut for winter feed for the animals. As well as cattle, pigs are kept in the Po Valley in the north, one of the top agricultural regions of Italy. Cured meats, such as salami and pancetta, are produced from pig meat. The city of Parma is known for Parma ham and for delicious Parmesan cheese, which is grated to garnish pasta, pizza, and soups.

In the fall, Italians gather porcini and other wild mushrooms in the woods. They may be sold fresh, dried, or bottled in oil, to be used in many dishes. The truffle is a rare type of mushroom that grows beneath the soil. Trained pigs or dogs sniff out these mushrooms so that they can be collected.

DID YOU KNOW?

Truffles grow underground near trees, which provide nutrients to help them grow. But in ancient Greece, people believed that truffles grew where lightning struck the moist earth!

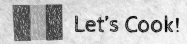
Grain and Grapes

The fertile Po Valley is Italy's richest agricultural region and is sometimes called "Food Valley." Corn, rice, wheat, beets, fruits, and vegetables all grow here. Wheat is milled to make many types of pasta, and cornmeal is boiled to make a dish called polenta, which is like cornmeal mush. The short-grain rice grown here is used in mouthwatering risotto dishes, made with cream and vegetables.

Wine grapes are cultivated in different regions of Italy, and the soil affects the taste of each. Some wines are made just for the family or area, but most are produced for international export. Regions famous for fine wines include Veneto, Tuscany, Umbria, Piedmont, Lombardy, and Emilia-Romagna.

Juicy purple grapes ripen in a vineyard. Italy is famous for its red wines.

Olive Orchards

Olive trees have been grown in the Mediterranean for thousands of years. Many regions in Italy have the perfect growing conditions, including Calabria, Puglia, Sicily, and Sardinia. Italy produces an amazing 3 million tons of olives per year! Some are salted in brine and eaten on their own or used as an ingredient in cooking. But most of the olives grown are pressed to make olive oil, the main fat used in Italian cuisine. Mixed with basil and pine nuts, olive oil makes a fragrant pasta sauce.

Olive trees grow in a grove in Florence. The trees are cultivated widely in Italy.

Zesty Citrus

The island of Sicily is famous for its citrus fruit, including oranges, lemons, mandarins, citron, and blood oranges. (Blood oranges have red flesh and a richer taste than some "orange" oranges.) Sicilian lemons are enormous and very juicy. The juice is used in salad dressings, and lemons are used in many desserts. *Granita siciliana* is a semifrozen iced dessert made with lemon juice, sugar, and water. It can also be made in flavors such as mandarin, chocolate, and jasmine!

Lemons are an important ingredient in Italian cuisine. The juice mixed with olive oil makes a tangy salad dressing.

Let's Cook!

Let's Start Cooking

One thing's for sure—cooking is a lot of fun! In this book, you will learn about different ingredients, which tastes go together, and new cooking methods. Some recipes have steps that you'll need help with, so you can ask a parent or another adult. When your delicious meal is ready, you can serve it to family and friends.

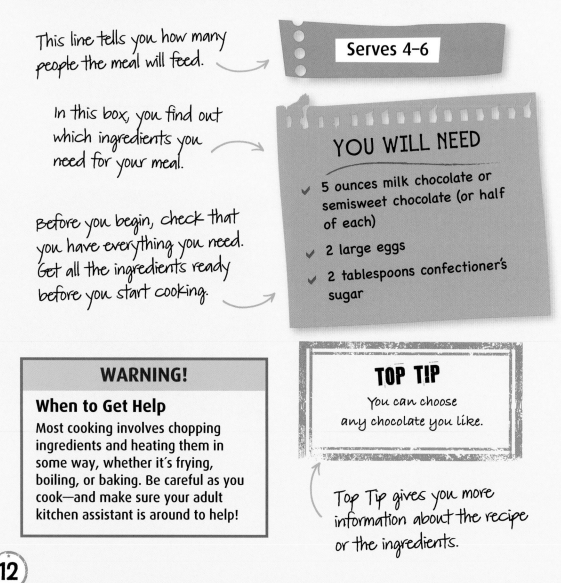

This line tells you how many people the meal will feed.

Serves 4-6

In this box, you find out which ingredients you need for your meal.

YOU WILL NEED

- 5 ounces milk chocolate or semisweet chocolate (or half of each)
- 2 large eggs
- 2 tablespoons confectioner's sugar

Before you begin, check that you have everything you need. Get all the ingredients ready before you start cooking.

WARNING!

When to Get Help

Most cooking involves chopping ingredients and heating them in some way, whether it's frying, boiling, or baking. Be careful as you cook—and make sure your adult kitchen assistant is around to help!

TOP TIP

You can choose any chocolate you like.

Top Tip gives you more information about the recipe or the ingredients.

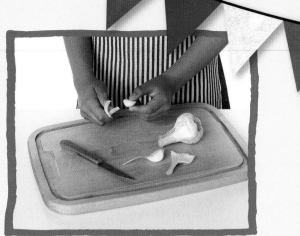

For many meals, you need to chop an onion. Cut a thin slice off at both ends, then pull off the papery skin. Cut the onion in half down the middle. Put one half, cut side down, on the cutting board. Hold it with one hand, and cut slices with the other hand. Hold the slices together, then cut across them to make small cubes. Be careful not to cut yourself!

Some recipes in this book use fresh garlic. Take a whole head of garlic, and break it into separate cloves. Cut the top and the bottom off each clove, and pull off the papery skin. You can chop the garlic clove with a sharp knife, or use a garlic press to crush the garlic directly into a skillet or saucepan.

METRIC CONVERSIONS

Oven Temperature		Liquid		Sugar	
°F	°C	Cups	Milliliters	Cups	Grams
275	140	¼	60	¼	50
300	150	½	120	½	100
325	170	¾	180	¾	150
350	180	1	240	1	200
375	190				
400	200	Weight		Flour	
425	220	Ounces	Grams	Cups	Grams
450	230	1	30	¼	30
475	240	2	60	½	60
		3	85	¾	90
		4	115	1	120
		5	140		
		6	175		
		7	200		
		8	225		

Minestrone

Serves 4

Minestrone is a hearty and delicious soup that calls for lots of vegetables! Served with Italian bread, it makes a warming winter meal.

YOU WILL NEED

- 2 pounds waxy potatoes
- 2 pounds mixed vegetables and beans (for example, cannellini beans, green beans, zucchini, celery, carrots, broccoli, lima beans)
- 10 ounces tomatoes
- 1 onion
- 3 ounces pancetta (optional)
- 2 tablespoons olive oil
- 1 garlic clove
- 2 pints vegetable stock
- 1 cup uncooked small pasta shapes
- ½ bunch parsley
- 1½ bunches basil
- salt, black pepper
- 4 tablespoons pesto
- 2 ounces pecorino or Parmesan cheese

1 Wash and peel the potatoes, then cut them into small cubes. Wash and trim the other vegetables. Cut them into small pieces, too. Drain the beans. Place the tomatoes in a bowl, and pour hot water over them. Leave for 1 minute, then rinse in cold water.

TOP TIP

Pancetta is an Italian bacon made from the belly of a pig. If you want to make meat-free minestrone, just leave it out.

2 Pull off the tomato skins, then halve and deseed the tomatoes. Carefully cut out the woody centers, and cut the tomato flesh into cubes. Chop the onion (see page 13), and cube the pancetta.

3 In a big saucepan, heat the oil. Add the pancetta. Fry until the fat starts to run, then add the onions. Fry, stirring from time to time, until the onions turn golden yellow. Do not let them burn.

4 Peel and chop the garlic, and add to the saucepan. Add all the other vegetables and beans, but hold back the tomatoes.

5 Fry for 2–3 minutes, stirring from time to time. Add the stock, and bring to a boil. Stir in the cubed tomatoes, and turn the heat to low. Add the pasta, stirring. Simmer for about 20 minutes.

6 Roughly chop the herbs, and stir into the minestrone. Season the soup with salt and pepper, then ladle into individual bowls. Serve with a spoonful of pesto and freshly grated cheese.

Pasta Sauces

Makes 2 sauces

These pasta sauce recipes are both delicious!
One uses fragrant basil, the other is a classic sauce
with meat. Serve with spaghetti or other pasta.

YOU WILL NEED

TO MAKE PESTO

- 2 ounces pine nuts
- 3 or 4 handfuls basil, plus extra leaves to garnish
- 3 garlic cloves
- salt, black pepper
- 7 tablespoons cold-pressed olive oil
- 2 ounces Parmesan cheese

1 Put a dry skillet on low heat, and fry the pine nuts. Stir until they start to turn brown, then take out immediately. Pull the leaves off the basil, and peel the garlic cloves.

2 Using a hand blender or a mixer, blend all the ingredients to make a smooth paste. Mix the pesto into cooked pasta.

YOU WILL NEED

TO MAKE BOLOGNESE

- ✓ 3 ounces smoked bacon
- ✓ 1 onion
- ✓ 1 garlic clove
- ✓ 1 carrot
- ✓ 1 stick celery
- ✓ 3 tablespoons olive oil
- ✓ 1 pound ground beef
- ✓ 2 tablespoons chopped parsley
- ✓ 1 pinch ground cloves
- ✓ salt, black pepper
- ✓ 2 cups beef or chicken stock
- ✓ 1½ pounds canned tomatoes (peeled and chopped)
- ✓ basil leaves, to garnish

1 Cut the bacon into small cubes. Peel the onion and the garlic, and chop both (see page 13). Peel the carrot, and trim the celery stick. Cube them both.

2 In a large saucepan, heat the olive oil. Add the bacon, onion, garlic, carrot, and celery. Fry for 5 minutes, stirring from time to time.

3 Now add the ground beef, and fry until the meat has turned brown. Break up any clumps as you go. Add the parsley, cloves, salt, and pepper, and stir. Pour in the stock. Add the tomatoes, stirring again. Boil the sauce on low. Cover with a lid, and let the pan simmer for at least 3 hours.

4 Check the sauce from time to time, and stir. If it seems too thick, add a little stock. Serve hot with pasta, garnished with basil leaves.

Tomato Risotto

Serves 4

Risotto is a rice-based dish from northern Italy. This recipe uses tangy sundried tomatoes, but others use vegetables such as asparagus or peas.

YOU WILL NEED

- ✓ 1 onion
- ✓ 1 tablespoon butter
- ✓ 3 tablespoons olive oil
- ✓ 1 1/4 cups risotto rice
- ✓ 2 3/4 cups beef or chicken stock
- ✓ 4 ounces sundried tomatoes in oil
- ✓ 1 large bunch mixed herbs
- ✓ 2 tablespoons pine nuts
- ✓ salt, black pepper
- ✓ 4 tablespoons freshly grated pecorino cheese
- ✓ fennel sprigs and olives, to garnish

1 Peel and chop the onion (see page 13). Heat the butter and the olive oil in a saucepan. When it begins to foam, add the onion. Stir-fry for about 3 minutes, until the onion becomes transparent (looks glassy).

2 Pour in the risotto rice, then stir until all the grains are coated with oil.

TOP TIP

When you make risotto, use Arborio, Vialone, or Carnaroli rice. All these rices have big, short, round grains, and they can soak up lots of liquid.

3 Pour in the stock, a little at a time. Stir and cook each time until the stock has been absorbed (the mixture starts to look dry). Keep adding more stock.

4 Finely chop the sundried tomatoes. Then wash the herbs, and shake them dry. Throw away any thick stems and yellow leaves. Roughly chop the leaves.

5 Heat a skillet without oil, and stir in the pine nuts. Roast them, and keep stirring to prevent burning. Remove the pan from the heat as soon as the pine nuts start to brown.

6 When the rice is almost done, stir the herbs and tomatoes into the pan. Season with salt and pepper, stir, and cook for a few minutes. The risotto should be moist but not sloppy. Sprinkle with the pine nuts and grated cheese. To serve, garnish with fennel and olives.

Let's Cook!
National Festivals

Italy knows how to throw a party! People celebrate 11 national holidays per year, plus seasonal and religious holidays, too.

Fairy-Tale Carnival

Carnevale (which means "farewell to meat") is the festival celebrated before the Roman Catholic 40-day fast of Lent begins. It is held in many towns throughout Italy, but the most famous one is in Venice. The Carnival of Venice is centuries old and began as a celebration of a military victory. No one is sure why, but people started wearing elaborate and colorful masks to Carnival—and even in everyday life! Today, tourists from around the world visit Venice to join in the fun. There are tightrope walkers, masked balls, and other exciting events. *Martedi Grasso* (Shrove or "Fat" Tuesday) is the last day of the festival, the day before Ash Wednesday.

Partygoers wear traditional costumes with masks at the Venice Carnival, in St. Mark's Square.

Colomba di Pasqua ("Easter dove") is a traditional cake. It is made in the shape of a dove to represent the Holy Spirit.

Easter Ecstasy

When Lent is over, people prepare to celebrate Easter, the day that Christians believe Jesus Christ rose from the dead. About 80 percent of Italians are Catholic, and most attend a solemn mass on Good Friday. Church bells ring at 3:00 p.m. out of respect for the time that Jesus died on the cross. On Holy Saturday, the day before Easter, an Easter Vigil (a time of prayer) is held—this is the holiest day of the year.

Easter Sunday is marked with feasting and celebrations. People greet each other gaily, saying *Buon Pasqua* ("Happy Easter"). Large family meals include a lamb roast (which symbolizes Jesus), vegetables, pasta, and eggs. Eggs are an important part of Easter, too: they symbolize springtime and new life. Children have fun painting eggs in bright colors and going on Easter egg hunts for real or chocolate eggs.

DID YOU KNOW?

For Carnival, people eat fritters that have many strange names. They are called Cenci (tatters), Donzelli (young ladies), Lattughe (lettuce), Nastri delle Suore (nuns' ribbons), Crostoli (crusts), and Chiacchere (gossip)!

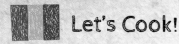

A nativity scene is set up in homes all across Italy in early December.

DID YOU KNOW?

Christmas in Italy continues until the Epiphany on January 6. This is the day Italians exchange presents.

Christmas Joy

In Italy, the Christmas season starts on December 8, when families set up a nativity scene, or crèche, in each home. Children take great care putting together little statues of Mary, Joseph, and the baby Jesus in a manger, or crib, surrounded by the wise men, angels, and animals. Many nativity scenes are made from beautiful materials and fabrics, and are passed down through families. Italians eat their main Christmas meal on Christmas Eve. It often includes fish, vegetables, and bread and olives, but no meat. For dessert, light, buttery cakes called panettone and pandoro are enjoyed, along with honey and nut sweets called torrone.

Fireworks are set off over St. Peter's Square in Vatican City to celebrate Christmas.

Regional Festivals

Festivals in Italy include some unusual customs. In Ivrea, the Battle of the Oranges carnival is celebrated with townspeople splitting up into nine teams and throwing oranges at each other! The festival has a bloody history commemorating a battle dating back to the twelfth century.

Medieval festivals, such as jousting contests and horse racing, recall a time when local clans fought each other. Hundreds of food festivals give Italians a chance to get together and sample local specialties. In central Italy especially, arts festivals are popular in the summer. They may feature a famous local composer in a series of concerts or operas, which are sometimes performed in ancient outdoor amphitheaters.

People pelt each other with fruit at the Battle of the Oranges carnival in Ivrea.

Lamb Roast

Serves 4–6

Lamb is the main attraction at any Easter Sunday family meal. Often, a number of delicious savory courses are served, followed by desserts.

YOU WILL NEED

- 1 small leg of lamb (about 3½ pounds)
- 4 garlic cloves
- 2–3 tablespoons fresh thyme leaves
- 6 tablespoons olive oil
- salt, black pepper
- 3½ cups vegetable stock
- 1½ pounds new potatoes
- 2 large onions
- 1½ pounds zucchini
- 2 red bell peppers
- 2 yellow bell peppers

1 Preheat the oven to 480°F. Pat the lamb dry if it is moist. Peel the garlic (see page 13), and cut each clove into thin slivers.

2 With a sharp knife, make little cuts in the meat, and stuff a garlic sliver into each one. Wash the thyme, and carefully pull the leaves off the stems. Mix the olive oil, salt, pepper, and thyme in a small bowl, and rub this all over the lamb skin.

3 Put the lamb in a roasting pan and put in the oven for about 20 minutes.

4 Wearing oven mitts, take the pan out of the oven, and add half of the stock. Reduce the heat to 400°F. Put the lamb back in the oven, and cook for another 40 minutes.

5 Wash and peel the potatoes. Peel the onions, and wash and trim the zucchini. Then wash, trim, and deseed the bell peppers. Cut the onions and all the vegetables into strips or chunks. Remove the lamb from the oven again, and add the vegetables and the rest of the stock.

6 Put the pan back in the oven, and cook the lamb for another 60 minutes. Remove from the oven, arrange the lamb and vegetables on a platter, and serve.

TOP TIP

Stuffed artichokes and lemon and asparagus pasta are served with Easter lamb, too. The table is often decorated with fresh flowers and colorfully dyed eggs!

Panettone

Makes 8–10 pieces of cake

Christmas in Italy always needs a large, sweet panettone! This light, airy, buttery cake is a hit with all ages, from *bambini* (children) to grandparents.

YOU WILL NEED

- 1½ packages active dry yeast
- 2/3 cup lukewarm milk
- 1 teaspoon sugar
- 3½ cups all-purpose flour
- 5 egg yolks
- 1 pinch salt
- 2/3 cup softened butter
- 2/3 cup dried fruit (raisins, dates, figs, candied lemon or orange rind)
- 5/8 cup chopped almonds (optional)

PLUS:
- butter for greasing and flour for the mold
- confectioner's sugar, to dust

1 Put the yeast in a bowl. Pour in a little milk, and stir until smooth. Stir in the sugar and a little flour. Take a clean dishcloth and cover the bowl, then leave it for 10–15 minutes.

2 In a large bowl, combine the yeast mixture with the rest of the milk, and add the flour, egg yolks, salt, and butter. Wash and dry your hands, then knead the ingredients together until you have a smooth dough. Cover with a dishcloth, and leave in a warm place for 1 hour.

DID YOU KNOW?

In traditional Italian recipes, panettone dough is left to rise three times. This makes the cake light and fluffy. But it takes several days to make this way. Luckily, the fast version is just as yummy!

3 Make a ring of foil, and place it around the inside of a large round springform cake pan 8 inches (20 cm) in diameter. The edge of the foil should come up higher than the pan. Put a little softened butter on a paper towel, and grease the inside of the pan and foil. Dust both with flour.

4 Preheat the oven to 400°F. Chop the dried fruit, and knead into the dough along with the almonds. Carefully lift the dough into the pan. Cover with a clean dishcloth, and let it rise for 30 minutes.

5 Bake the cake on the lowest shelf for 45 minutes, until it is golden brown. Remove from the oven, and let it cool in the pan for 20 minutes. Then gently lift the cake out of the pan, and put it on a wire rack. Cover with a dishcloth, and leave until it has cooled completely.

6 To finish, put a little confectioner's sugar in a small strainer, dust the top of the panettone with it, and serve!

Celebrating at Home

In Italy, people spend special occasions such as birthdays, baptisms, and weddings with the entire family. Friends and neighbors often join in the celebrations, too!

Wedding Bells

An Italian wedding is a major celebration that includes family, friends, and the whole community. On the night before the ceremony, it is considered good luck for the bride to wear green. But she must not look at herself in the mirror before putting on her dress in the morning! Outside the church, the groom hands the bride a bouquet to show that he is willing to marry. Then the couple pass under a bowed ribbon at the church doorway. This symbolizes that they are about to "tie the knot." After the ceremony, the reception features music, dancing, and a huge feast, including a lavish cake. The guests are given "confetti," which are party favors consisting of 5 or 7 candy-coated almonds. The odd number means that the couple can never be divided in two.

A four-layer wedding cake is decorated with fancy frosting and fresh flowers.

A wedding ceremony is celebrated in a cathedral in Palermo, Sicily. The bride and groom stand at the altar.

Baptism Blessings

Traditionally, Italian babies baptized in the Catholic Church are given the name of the saint celebrated on their birthday. Before the ceremony, the parents choose godparents, who are responsible for the child's religious education. They send out invitations to the church service. There, the baby is sprinkled with holy water over a baptismal font and blessed by a priest. Afterward, a party takes place in the parents' home, where the baby is presented to family and friends. Homemade cakes and pastries are served—it is unlucky to serve store-bought baked goods for this occasion!

DID YOU KNOW?

In some parts of Italy, the bride and groom shatter a glass after their wedding. The shards of glass are said to represent the years of happiness they will share together in their married life.

Baptism is an important ceremony. It is when the baby is given a name.

Slow Food

In Italy, food is big news! People believe in taking a lot of time choosing or growing fresh ingredients, planning meals, and cooking family recipes. And when it is all prepared and on the table, they like to take time savoring their meal over talk with family and friends.

An official Slow Food organization was started in Italy by Carlo Petrini in the 1980s. The group aims to prevent fast-food restaurants from taking over local food traditions and enjoyment of leisurely meals. It also tries to preserve plants and animals that grow and live naturally in an area. The Slow Food movement has now spread to over 150 other countries worldwide.

An Italian family enjoys a leisurely lunch together, eating and chatting.

DID YOU KNOW?

The weather is hot and sunny for much of the Italian summer. Many families eat outside almost every night. This is called dining "al fresco" (meaning "in the open air").

Happy Birthdays

People's saint's (name) day used to be more important than their birthday in Italy. But today, birthdays are widely celebrated. Children invite their friends to a party, which often takes place outside. First, the birthday boy or girl opens their present and thanks each giver. Then the children take turns trying to break open a piñata, a decorated animal stuffed with candy and toys. Finally, the parents serve food, including panini (toasted sandwiches), *pizzettas* (little pizzas), and a scrumptious *torta* (a large, flat birthday cake)!

Children look forward to sharing a frosted *torta* at an outdoor birthday party.

Pizzettas are mini pizzas. They are often served at children's birthday parties.

Saltimbocca

Serves 4

This tender meat dish is made with veal cutlets and ham. It gets its aromatic flavor from the herb sage. The dish can also be made with chicken.

YOU WILL NEED

- 8 thin slices of veal cutlets or chicken breast (about 1 pound 2 ounces)
- white pepper
- 8 very thin slices of Parma ham
- 2 sprigs of sage
- 2 tablespoons butter or olive oil
- salt
- ½ cup vegetable stock
- thin cucumber slices, to garnish

1 Put the veal cutlets on a cutting board. Flatten them using a meat mallet or rolling pin. Season the meat with white pepper.

DID YOU KNOW?

Calves used to be kept in crates to produce veal, which was cruel to the animals. Only use pasture-raised veal, where the animals have been able to roam free.

2 Put one slice of Parma ham on each veal cutlet. Wash the sage and pat dry. Remove the leaves, and put one leaf on top of each Parma ham slice.

5 Lightly season the cutlets with salt. Place on a serving platter, and cover with foil. Keep the platter warm in an oven preheated to 200°F.

3 Using wooden toothpicks, pin the sage and ham slices to the veal cutlets, one at a time.

4 Heat the butter or olive oil in a large skillet until it starts to foam. Put the cutlets in the pan, and fry them for about 2 minutes, or until they are lightly browned. Turn them over, then fry for another 2 minutes.

6 To make gravy, pour the stock into the pan, stirring all the time. Taste, and add more pepper or salt if needed. Pour into a gravy boat, and serve with the cutlets. Garnish with cucumber slices and serve.

Cassata

Makes 1 cake

This scrumptious cake is often the highlight of a holiday feast! It comes from southern Italy and Sicily, and has many variations.

YOU WILL NEED

- ✓ 4 ounces semisweet chocolate
- ✓ 10–14 ounces mixed candied fruit
- ✓ 5 ounces sugar
- ✓ 5 drops vanilla
- ✓ juice of ½ orange
- ✓ 1¾ pounds ricotta cheese
- ✓ 3 round sponge cakes, 9 inches (22 cm) in diameter
- ✓ 8 fluid ounces whipping cream

1 Chop the semisweet chocolate into fine pieces using a sharp knife. Then chop 5 ounces of the candied fruit.

DID YOU KNOW?

Candied fruit is crystallized. Fruit is dipped into hot sugar syrup several times and left to dry between each dipping. This method of preserving fruit keeps it edible for longer.

2 In a small saucepan, stir the sugar into 7 tablespoons of water. Bring to a boil, stirring all the time. Continue cooking over medium heat, and keep stirring until the liquid turns into a light syrup. Take the pan off the heat. Stir in the vanilla and orange juice, and let the syrup cool a little.

4 Put one sponge cake on a platter, and place a 9-inch (22 cm) springform cake pan ring around the base. Spread half the creamed ricotta on top with a spoon, then add a second sponge cake on top. Spread the rest of the ricotta on this, then cover with the last sponge cake. Chill.

3 In a large bowl, beat the ricotta with a wooden spoon until it is creamy. Add the sugar syrup, then add the chopped chocolate and candied fruit. Stir well to combine.

5 Remove the cake ring. Then whip the whipping cream using a whisk or hand blender until it is stiff. Using a plastic spatula, spread the whipped cream over the top and sides of the cassata. Arrange candied fruit slices in a pattern on top, and serve.

Daily Life in Italy

In the north, most Italians live in the towns and cities, where industry is focused. But in the south, many people work on farms and in vineyards. Wherever they live, Italians all cherish family life.

Different Homes

In big cities such as Rome, Milan, and Naples, families tend to live in apartments rather than houses. Many large, old houses in downtown areas have been converted into elegant and expensive apartments. In the countryside and small villages, where there is more space, people live in one-family houses. Many Italian families have only one child, so most young people live at home until they get married. Their parents often help them to buy or rent an apartment nearby.

Downtown Rome has many old houses that have been split up and turned into modern apartments.

Cheeses, salamis, antipasti, and other deli foods are eaten for lunch on hot days in Italy.

Lunch and Snooze

Because Italy's weather is hot for much of the year, everything stops for a few hours in the afternoon. Schools, offices, and stores close at 1:00 p.m., and most people go home to eat lunch with their families. They may have a pasta dish (*primo piatto*), followed by a meat or fish dish (*secundo piatto*) served with salad. On very hot days, antipasti—cold meats, seafood, and vegetables—is eaten.

After lunch, everyone rests. This is called *riposo*, meaning "rest," and is like a Mexican siesta. Shops and offices stay closed until 4:00 p.m., so there is time for people to sleep. Children stay indoors even if they don't sleep, so that they don't disturb others with noisy games.

DID YOU KNOW?

Most Italians go on vacation in their own country. They escape the heat of the cities to visit seaside resorts or the mountains. People tend to vacation in August, when offices and schools close.

A family spends some quiet time together on a beach in the afternoon.

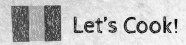

Families stroll together ➡
in the evening on the
streets of downtown Siena.

Time to Play

Italians love to socialize! Instead of
watching TV or playing computer
games after dinner, they like to walk
around their neighborhood or downtown
and chat with people. This is called the
passeggiata. Whole families often
stroll together until midnight on hot
summer nights. They usually dress in
nice clothes, as they enjoy looking
good and being fashionable.

The most popular sport in Italy is
calcio, or soccer. Fans avidly follow
their favorite teams. At the games,
they wear and paint their faces with
team colors. Basketball is another
favorite sport popularized by the
United States after World War II.
Cycling is a widespread sport; local
clubs and international teams cause
a lot of excitement on the road.

⭐ DID YOU KNOW?

Italo Marchioni, an
ice cream vendor who
emigrated from Italy to
New York, invented the
ice cream cone in 1896. ⭐

People eat outdoors at
a restaurant in Ravello,
on the Amalfi Coast.

School Days

Free education is available for all children in Italy. At six years old, they start school and attend elementary school until the age of 11. From 11 to 14 years old, they go to middle school. Then at 14, they attend high school for three to five years. Students can choose classes based around technical skills, science, classical studies, teacher training, and language. Most schools run for six days a week, Monday to Saturday! The school day starts early at 8:30 a.m. and finishes at around 1:00 p.m.

Eating Out

Italians enjoy eating out, and Italy has some of the best restaurants in Europe. People also take their families for dinner at pizzerias, which have a healthy and flavorful selection of salads and pizzas. The *gelateria* (ice cream parlor) is a favorite of children and adults alike.

Antipasto

Serves 4

This tangy appetizer will whet your appetite before a meal! Marinated peppers are one of many antipasto dishes you can serve.

YOU WILL NEED

- 4 bell peppers

FOR THE DRESSING:
- 2 garlic cloves
- 1 tablespoon fresh thyme
- 6 tablespoons olive oil
- 3 tablespoons balsamic vinegar
- 1 tablespoon runny honey
- salt, black pepper
- basil leaves, to garnish

1 Preheat the oven to 480°F. Cut the bell peppers in half lengthwise. Remove the stalks and the white piths, then scrape out the seeds.

> ## TOP TIP
> More ideas for antipasti include: sundried tomatoes on bread; goat cheese on crackers; salami slices; marinated mushrooms; and spicy olives.

2 Wash the pepper halves, and put them with rounded side up on the baking sheet. Bake in the preheated oven for 10–15 minutes, until the skin turns black and blisters.

3 Remove from the oven, and cover the peppers with a clean, damp dishcloth. Let them cool until you can touch them without burning your fingers.

4 Using a knife, pull off the burned skin, and throw it away. Cut the peppers into strips 1 inch (2.5 cm) wide.

5 Peel and crush the garlic into a small bowl (see page 13). Then add the thyme, olive oil, vinegar, honey, salt, and pepper. Stir all ingredients to combine.

6 Place the pepper strips on a platter, and drizzle the marinade over the top. Cover with plastic wrap, and leave to stand for at least 4 hours in a cool place.

7 Uncover the peppers, and place on individual plates. Garnish with the basil leaves, and serve.

Margherita Pizza

Serves 4

Pizza is one of the most popular foods on Earth. You can make it with many toppings, but this simple cheese and tomato recipe is a classic!

YOU WILL NEED

FOR THE BASE:
- 1 package active dry yeast
- 1 pinch sugar
- 4 cups white bread flour
- 4 tablespoons olive oil
- 1 teaspoon salt

FOR THE TOPPING:
- 1 large can peeled tomatoes
- ½ pound mozzarella cheese
- salt, black pepper
- handful of olives (optional)
- 4 tablespoons grated Parmesan cheese
- 4 tablespoons olive oil, plus extra for brushing and drizzling
- 1 to 2 handfuls fresh basil

1 Sprinkle the yeast into a bowl, then stir in 5 tablespoons lukewarm water and the sugar. Add 3 tablespoons flour, and stir. Cover with a dishcloth, and let stand for 20 minutes in a warm place.

2 Add the rest of the flour, the olive oil, salt, and ¾ cup lukewarm water. Knead together with your hands until the dough is smooth. Cover with a dishcloth. Let stand in a warm place for 60 minutes.

3 Preheat the oven to 480°F. Line up four pizza pans 8 inches (20 cm) in diameter, and brush with oil. Divide the dough into four, then roll each piece into a flat, round disk. Put in pizza pans.

TOP TIP

For a thicker crust, double the base ingredients, and roll the dough out thicker. Bake pizzas at 400°F for 15 minutes.

4 Drain the can of tomatoes in a sieve, and spread them across the pizza bases. Squash them a bit with a fork. Leave 1 inch (2.5 cm) of pizza dough uncovered all around the edges.

5 Cut the mozzarella into thin slices, and put them evenly on the pizzas. Season with salt and pepper. Scatter the olives across, if using. Sprinkle the pizza with Parmesan, and drizzle with olive oil.

6 Bake the pizzas, one after another, on the middle shelf in the oven for 8–10 minutes. Garnish with basil leaves, and serve.

Tiramisu

Serves 4

This creamy dessert was invented in the region around Venice. *Tiramisu* means "pick-me-up." Once you taste it, you'll agree it does just that!

YOU WILL NEED

- 2 fresh egg yolks
- 2 tablespoons sugar
- ½ pound mascarpone
- 1 teaspoon grated zest of an untreated lemon
- ½ cup hot chocolate, cooled
- 1 package ladyfinger cookies
- 1 tablespoon cocoa powder
- small amaretti cookies and chocolate decoration (optional)

1 Place the egg yolks and sugar, along with 4 tablespoons of hot water, into a bowl. Beat the ingredients with a hand mixer for 5 minutes, or until it is thick and creamy.

2 Add the mascarpone, a spoonful at a time, to the egg mixture. Stir it in with a fork. Then add the lemon zest, stirring to mix evenly. Next, pour the hot chocolate into a shallow dish.

5 Cover the tiramisu dish with plastic wrap or a clean dishcloth. Chill in the refrigerator for 3 hours. Decorate with amaretti cookies and a chocolate decoration, if you like. Before serving, dust with cocoa powder.

3 Dip ladyfinger cookies, one by one, in the hot chocolate. Cover the base of a second shallow dish with them.

4 Using a rubber spatula, spread half the mascarpone cheese on top of cookies. Smooth the layer with the back of a spoon. Then dip the remaining cookies in hot chocolate, and place on top of the mascarpone layer. Spread these with more mascarpone. Smooth and even out the top.

TOP TIP

Mascarpone is a fresh cream cheese made from the milk of cows fed on a special diet. You can make tiramisu with ricotta instead, though. Just whip it with a fork until it's very smooth.

Glossary

antipasto An Italian appetizer. Many different small pieces of food are counted as antipasti, from marinated peppers, mushrooms, and eggplant to salami and ham slices.

bolognese A tomato-based meat sauce in the style typical of Bologna, a town in northern Italy.

confetti (1) Small slivers of paper thrown at weddings; (2) a bag of candy-coated almonds given as favors on special occasions in Italy.

granita siciliana A semifrozen dessert from Sicily, usually made with lemon juice, sugar, and water.

mascarpone A triple-cream cheese from Lombardy. It is white and easy to spread and an important ingredient in the dessert tiramisu.

pancetta An Italian fatty bacon, cured and spiced, and usually rolled.

panettone A tall Italian cake that is served during the Christmas holidays. It is made with flour, butter, sugar, yeast, and candied fruit.

parmesan A hard cheese from Parma, in northern Italy. It is often grated over pasta dishes and soups at the table.

passeggiata A stroll that Italian families take through town in the evening after dinner.

pesto A cold pasta sauce made from basil leaves, garlic, oil, and pine nuts.

prosciutto A northern Italian dry-cured ham. The best known is Parma ham; it is usually cut into very thin slices.

riposo The Italian word for "siesta," a period of rest after lunch during which stores and schools are closed.

risotto A dish from northern Italy made with rice cooked in stock with added vegetables, meat, or poultry.

saltimbocca A dish made from veal cutlets, fried with prosciutto and sage.

tiramisu A dessert made from coffee, brandy, mascarpone, ladyfinger cookies, and cocoa. The children's version leaves out the coffee and brandy.

vigil A time to stay awake when people are usually asleep, especially to watch and pray; the eve of a holy day.

Further Resources

Books

James, Simon.
DK Eyewitness Books: Ancient Rome.
DK Children's Books, New York: 2015.

Lonely Planet.
Not For Parents Rome: Everything You Ever Wanted to Know.
Lonely Planet, Oakland, CA: 2011.

Prandoni, Anna.
Let's Cook Italian: A Family Cookbook.
Quarry Books, Beverly, MA: 2015.

Throp, Claire.
Italy (Countries Around the World).
Heinemann, Portsmouth, NH: 2011.

Websites

Due to the changing nature of Internet links, PowerKids Press has developed an online list of websites related to the subject of this book. This site is updated regularly. Please use this link to access the list:

www.powerkidslinks.com/lc/italy

Index